Joseph

The harsh reality of one's life

by
Louis R T Mulholland

MAPLE
PUBLISHERS

Joseph – The harsh reality of one's life

Author: Louis R T Mulholland

Copyright © 2023 Louis R T Mulholland

The right of Louis R T Mulholland to be identified as author of this work has been asserted by the author in accordance with section 77 and 78 of the Copyright, Designs and Patents Act 1988.

First Published in 2023

ISBN 978-1-83538-116-8 (Paperback)
     978-1-83538-117-5 (Hardback)
     978-1-83538-118-2 (E-Book)

Book Cover Design and Book Layout by:
     White Magic Studios
     www.whitemagicstudios.co.uk

Published by:
     Maple Publishers
     Fairbourne Drive, Atterbury,
     Milton Keynes,
     MK10 9RG, UK
     www.maplepublishers.com

Joseph

Joseph Carey Merrick was born in the Nineteenth Century and by all accounts given by his friends and by the staff at London Hospital, he was a kind soul who had a big heart for everyone he came in contact with. He was a very intelligent man who loved everything creative and dabbled in the creative side of many projects whilst living at the hospital. When Joseph died on 11th April 1890 at age 27, he had accumulated many friends. Some friends were members of the royal family, actors and actresses, musicians, surgeons, and nurses living at London Hospital. At first, these friends were fascinated by the appearance of Joseph and that's probably why all of them wanted to meet Joseph. It was only after sitting down and chatting to Joseph that they realized he was not incompetent and in fact was just like everybody else; his deformities did not in any way affect his personality. This is when they got to understand Joseph, realizing he was a lot more insightful and intelligent than many people, up to that point, had given him credit for. In fact, he was a delight to be around with his warm nature, generosity, polite mannerisms, and overall kind heart, resulting in people wanting to spend time with him. He formed friendships with many of the staff at the London Hospital who cared for him. These friendships usually began when they found Joseph wandering the grounds of his living quarters in the evenings. The staff would stop and chat with him when they encountered Joseph - sometimes having in-depth conversations but all the while feeling at ease and comfortable around him. The staff began looking forward to seeing him on other occasions. This is the main reason he became loved by many members of staff who in the end spoke highly of Joseph. Despite Joseph's own belief that his deformities had been the result of his mother's encounter with an elephant whilst pregnant which had escaped from a circus and got spooked, trampling over her to flee, the actual causes have been a subject of much discussion since his death.

Initially considered to be the result of 'Elephantiasis' (Elephantiasis is the enlargement and hardening of limbs or body parts due to tissue swelling), new tests since then have been undertaken. The disorder is now thought to be an extremely severe case of 'Neurofibromatosis' - a group of genetic disorders that cause tumours to form on nerve tissue. These tumours can develop anywhere in the nervous system, including the brain, spinal cord, and nerves. According to medical professionals, this is the most probable cause of the disorder for Joseph.

Brief Family History

- Barnabas Merrick Born 2nd September 1792 in Spitalfields, Middlesex, England was the grandfather of Joseph Merrick.

- Barnabas Merrick married firstly, Ann Bowen at Wanstead, Essex, England, on the 18th of July 1815. They had three children, John Barnabas born in 1816, William George born in 1818, then Mary Barnabas born in 1826.

- Barnabas later remarried a woman called Sarah Jones in London, England, on the 3rd of June 1826. They had no children.

- Barnabas remarried for a third time, a woman named Sarah Rockley at St. Peter's Church in Radford, Nottinghamshire, England, on the 19th of March 1837. They had three children, Joseph born in 1838 (father of Joseph Merrick), Henry born in 1841, and finally, Charles born in 1846 (who would later in life save Joseph from homelessness allowing his nephew to live with him and his wife for a brief period).

- Barnabas Merrick passed away in Leicester, Leicestershire, England, in 1856.

- Sarah Merrick born in 1803 in Burton Joyce, Nottinghamshire, England, United Kingdom was the grandmother to Joseph Merrick.

- Sarah Rockley married Barnabas Merrick, as his third spouse, at St. Peter's Church in Radford, Nottinghamshire, England, United Kingdom, under the Anglican faith, on the 19th of March 1837.

- There are no records of Sarah Rockley apart from her marriage to Barnabas. This is probably because the records don't date back that long with her being female. Her parents are listed as unknown.

- Her death was given as, Sarah found dead in Leicester Chronicle. Date as 7th February 1897.

- Joseph Merrick's father was the eldest Son of Barnabas Merrick and Sarah Rockley Merrick.

- He was born in 1838 in Leicestershire, England, United Kingdom.

- Joseph Rockley Merrick made his living as the driver of a brougham, a closed four-wheeled cab.

- Joseph Rockley Merrick met Mary Jane Potterton sometime in 1860 and they married at the Parish church of Thurmaston on 29th December 1861.

- Mary was already pregnant with Joseph when she walked down the altar.

- Mary Jane Potterton was herself born with a physical disability in 1839. She was born in the small village of Evington on the outskirts of Leicester, England.

- She was the third child in a big family of nine other siblings. Her parents, William, and Elizabeth Potterton were easygoing country people. Her father worked on a farm but could not read or write and had very little education growing up.

- When Mary Jane was about five her family relocated from Evington to settle in the village of Thurmaston. At twelve she left home to become a servant to a family in Leicester, she remained here for the next thirteen years enduring a life of long hours and low pay. Then in 1860 when she was twenty-five, she met Joseph Rockley Merrick.

Childhood: 1862-1879

Joseph Merrick was born on August 5th, 1862, at 50 Lee Street in Leicester, England, to Joseph Rockley Merrick (1838 - 1897) and Mary Jane Potterton (1837 – 1873). Mary was already pregnant by the time she got married, giving birth to Joseph when she was twenty-six. Mary had a physical disability which meant she was unable to work, and she had to rely solely on her husband Joseph Rockley to bring in the income while she was a struggling stay-at-home mum. Wages in those days were very low, especially for individuals of low IQs. But luckily for Joseph Rockley, having given up work as a brougham driver after he married Mary, he was now working in one of the many cotton factories. The hours were long with shifts lasting from 8 AM to 7 PM in winter and from 6 AM to 6 PM in summer. There were no bank holidays permitted and even Boxing Day was regarded as a normal working day. But wages were better than where he was previously, with men being able to earn between 12s-15s (60-75p) a week. Joseph Rockley was somewhat more fortunate. Having a higher position than most meant a slightly higher wage package. By all accounts, Joseph Merrick, a healthy child showed no signs that anything would be wrong in the future. He did suffer from a mild case of smallpox at the age of three months, but this was very common for young babies as there was an epidemic of smallpox raging through Leicester at the time and continuing for the following year. Joseph however did manage to recover from this and continued to develop healthily.

Unfortunately, there were more serious problems to come for baby Joseph at the age of only twenty-one months. Joseph started developing swellings on his lips and a bony lump on his forehead, which, over the next few months grew larger, spreading outwards as a hard tumour into his right cheek until his upper lip was being pushed outwards by a huge protruding mound of flesh. He was also showing early stages of loosening of the skin which were rough in texture. Over the coming months and years, this continued to force its way outwards from beneath the upper lip and in time it was to protrude several inches in a snout, weighing three or four ounces. At some stage in his younger years (the date has never been made fully clear) his left arm began swelling and becoming enlarged, and then both his feet became significantly enlarged and grotesque letting off a hideous stench. The smell of his body odour could never seem to be shifted. No matter how often he bathed it grew fouler as he aged. By the age of four, his mother Mary gave birth to the couple's second child William Arthur Merrick who was born in January 1866. This meant the physically disabled Mary was now a stay-at-home mum for two young children and one (Joseph) with abnormal problems. That would have been difficult for Mary to cope with day by day. At age five Joseph started developing patches of abnormal lumpy, greyish skin across his body which later grew and played a sad role in his difficult life as well as this, on 28th September 1867, while Joseph was still aged five, his parents had their third child - a daughter named Marion Eliza Merrick. She was born with physical disabilities like her mother, and she was hard to cope with showing what we would today deem as challenging behaviour (she suffered from physical problems such as myelitis, seizures, and fits, along with other impairments). By the age of eight, sadly his younger brother William only aged four died of scarlet fever on 21st December 1870. He was buried a few days later, on Christmas day. This was a common illness amongst children, especially around the 1800s. It is a bacterial infection which is accompanied by sore throats and high fevers. By the age of ten, Joseph was covered from head to toe in severe deformities which covered ninety percent of his body with various bony and wild fleshy tumours which were growing rapidly. The only area completely unaffected were his genitals. Due to all the different sizes and weights of these growths forming all over his body at some point in his childhood (age unknown), he suffered a bad fall which caused a very damaging injury to his left hip. This later became infected and left him with lifelong joint problems and having a permanently lame left side, causing him to walk lopsided, pushing all his weight onto his right side which only added to his abnormal appearance. Three months before Joseph's eleventh birthday, his mother died of bronchial pneumonia (this is a life-threatening illness which causes people to have trouble breathing because their airways are constricted, so the lungs aren't getting enough oxygen). Mary Jane was young when she passed at only thirty-seven, on 19ᵗʰ May 1873. Joseph would later describe her passing as "the greatest sadness in my life". Joseph was very close to his mother, so her passing was absolutely devastating to him. Up to that point in his life, she had been his only close friend and caregiver, so it was an unfortunate time of life for Joseph to be deprived of her love and affection. Though he was always to carry her in his mind as an idealized but vivid memory, his mother was someone who had to him been the source of all the warmth and comfort he had ever known. For Joseph, the disaster marked the end of his childhood.

The now widowed Joseph Rockley was recently promoted in his job, but now being left with his full-time job as an engine driver and being in charge of running a haberdashery shop along with his two 'crippled' children was proving too hard for him. He was unable to turn to family with his father having passed away in 1856 and his mother working in the cotton factories barely making ends meet, so he decided to relocate and move into lodgings only some hundred yards from their property. This was a smaller area and smaller property in itself at 4 Wanslip Street, Leicester, England, and this is where he first met property owner Emma Wood Antill who was a twenty-nine-year-old widow with children of her own. The two quickly formed a relationship, moving in together, then married on 3ʳᵈ December 1874, just over a year since Mary Jane had passed away. Joseph was age twelve. It was Emma to whom Joseph Rockley entrusted the care of his son and daughter, but this woman was unlike his mother in so many ways, being extremely strict and harsh towards young Joseph. For Joseph, his father's remarriage was a distressing time and easily labelled him the outcast he had always felt he was. It also added to the extra stress of having to compete with his new stepbrothers and stepsisters for the affection and attention of his father but never being able to gain it back (or gain back the little affection his father had once shown him growing up). Instead now his father rejected him passing him off as ugly, lame, dumb and an embarrassment to the family and himself.

By thirteen, his deformities had gotten so bad that it forced him to leave school. His right arm was two or three times the size of his left, his feet were extremely deformed, his head was double the size of the average person, and his jaws were completely out of place, which made his facial expressions hard to read, and also restrained his vocal activities. It is unclear how long Joseph attended school. All we know is that he did attend for a period in his childhood and left at thirteen when it became too difficult to continue. This was a boarding school on Syston Street, not far from his father's workshop. Whether or not this was a pleasant experience has never been mentioned by Joseph, as he always kept that part of his childhood very secret, but with his many deformities and abnormalities one can only imagine the harsh reality he must have faced day to day with the cruel forms of language kids use against matters they don't understand.

Straight after leaving school his father and stepmother demanded that he earn a living for his keep at the lodge, threatening him that if he didn't make money he would be thrown out onto the streets. This fear of being made homeless must have been frightening for young Joseph because - one, he had never interacted with anyone outside his parents and siblings, and two, he knew the general public could be cruel to individuals such as Joseph. He would repeatedly run away from home as he wasn't treated affectionately by his stepmother or father. But he returned home each time when his father would find him, dragging him back home with Joseph kicking and screaming. With his now very visible abnormalities and difficulties, this was going to make finding work for him challenging. But against all odds, shortly after leaving school, he did manage to secure a job at a cigar shop which consisted of him rolling up, packaging, and manufacturing the cigars.

The little money he earnt from his job all went to his father and stepmother for board and he was left with absolutely nothing for himself. Unfortunately, not even a year into his job he was fired because his right deformed hand had become so huge and stiff that it was becoming heavy, making it impossible for him to continue rolling the cigars. This didn't sit well with his father and stepmother who were very displeased with Joseph's firing, so his father resorted to beating Joseph on many occasions for his lack of income and his stepmother wouldn't allow him to eat, instead locking him away in the attic for days without food. Joseph continued trying to find work but due to his growing deformities, nobody would hire him. It was around this time, in 1875/1876, when he was thirteen or fourteen, that his speech began to worsen, so much so that he could barely pronounce his words and when he was able to talk his voice was quiet, frail, and sloppy.

After a while, his father did manage to get Joseph a Hawker's license (a hawker's license was a working license which allowed that individual to be a door-to-door salesman). In this case, it was selling items from his father's shop, mainly gloves but also sometimes men's clothing or accessories. Yet again, unfortunately for Joseph, this job was short-lived because his job role was going door to door and interacting with the public - which first off, Joseph struggled with in general but secondly, on most occasions, before he had the opportunity to talk to anybody, his appearance frightened the mass majority, so people either slammed the door in his face or point blank refused to answer telling him to get off their properties. On the occasions when he would get the opportunity to talk to somebody, his speech made it extremely difficult for them to understand so he was left unable to sell items. Because of the lack of income on Joseph's behalf, the beatings from his father became a lot more brutal and a lot more frequent. So whenever he came home empty-handed, which was more often than not, his father was not afraid of giving him a good hiding with his walking stick. Then, once again, his stepmother banished him to be locked in the attic with an empty belly. This would become a repeated ritual for Joseph over the next 2 years. He wouldn't be able to get the money he needed, so on returning home he would get a beating and be sent to the attic. So on many occasions, Joseph could be found limping around the streets, searching for scraps of food from the back of alleyways or in bins, not wanting to return home. He was by this point becoming more aware of the financial burden he was on his family and thinking of a way he could get out of the horrific, abusive situation he found himself in. He knew that roaming the streets with his visible limp and abnormal looks was getting him nowhere and often enough he found himself the target of sneers and jibes from groups of people stopping to stare at him, calling out despicable names, which in time wound him up tightly, making him shut off from people around him.

In 1879, when he was seventeen, after many beatings and sleepless nights with an empty belly, being locked away and not able to interact with anybody, Joseph took the brave move and decided to leave home choosing to render himself homeless rather than stay under a roof where he was beaten, isolated and miserable. He was homeless for approximately two weeks. As with a lot of things in Joseph's younger days, it has never been talked about in detail where Joseph stayed or if he had any troubles on the street. All he said about this time was that he was homeless for roughly a two-week period. He never wanted to delve any deeper into the topic. Luckily for Joseph, his uncle Charles had heard he was homeless and decided to take his nephew into his home where he lived with his wife Jane. Before taking in their nephew, the lives of Charles Merrick and his wife had not been easy. In 1878, the year Joseph was to be found living on the streets by his uncle, the couple had already seen three of their five children die before the age of eighteen months. Nevertheless, they responded as any loving family relatives would once they heard of their nephew's troubles, both going out of their way to search on the streets until they found Joseph and brought him back to their home. After just over a year, compared to what Joseph was used to, it must have felt to him like a weight was off his shoulders. It was all bittersweet because Joseph knew he couldn't continue staying with them, especially with the new arrival of the couple's next child. Although they both showed Joseph love and gave him food without expecting money in return, after only a short stay of a year, Joseph with his kind nature for others started to feel like a burden on them. The little money he was making he was giving to his aunty and uncle even though on most occasions they would reject his offer and let him keep his earnings of the day. Unfortunately, whilst staying at his uncle's, his Hawker's license got revoked because there were so many occasions when his appearance and deformities were scaring the community. So he was unable to work and provide money once again, and not only that, people were becoming very cruel towards Joseph on a daily basis. Every time he ventured outside for whatever reason he was being harassed by crowds of passersby who wanted to get a glance of the deformed freak. Some would follow him pointing and shouting. His appearance attracted so much attention that the commissioners for Hackney Carriages, on the grounds of acting in the public good felt obliged to take action, knowing he needed protection against the general public. Out of options, he left his uncle's and decided to sign up for the Poor Law workhouse scheme.

The Poor Law Act of 1834 was a modern-day homeless shelter for the elderly, sick, disabled, and poor but with the disadvantage of having to work hard unpaid labour, early mornings, late nights, and minimal food to ensure your stay. It was run like a prison, which meant if jobs weren't completed on time or to the standards expected there were consequences and these usually meant beatings, long stays in the isolation unit, or no food, but for Joseph, a beating, isolation, or vile words of torment towards him was nothing he wasn't used to (Joseph did suffer harsh beatings on occasions due to him not being able to complete tasks set out because of the restrictions on his body caused by his deformities).

⸻⸻◆◗◆⸻⸻

Adulthood 1879-1886

On Monday morning, not long after Christmas day 1879, Joseph made his way over to the Poor Law scheme building. It was a very dull day with heavy rainfall and cold winds. Joseph arrived and introduced himself to relieving officer William Cartwright, who was one of the Board of Guardians responsible for administering the Poor Law. Joseph presented himself trying to articulate the best he could with his difficulty in communicating effectively, demonstrating his difficulties and deformities, and showing the officer why it was so hard for him to get and hold down permanent employment. William Cartwright found little reasoning on why not to offer Joseph a place and made his decision to grant Joseph his admission to the workhouse. On that very same morning, Joseph walked through the gates of the Leicester Union Workhouse and was shown around the building, then finally was taken to where he would be staying. Before being allocated to his new so-called home he first had to be escorted to the admission block for the ritual of registration. He stripped down, showered, and was handed workhouse clothes which were dull in colour and undistinguished in pattern. His clothes were stored away for when or if he might be discharged but not before pockets were emptied and any valuable belongings or money was confiscated (stolen) as a contribution to his keep. Finally, Joseph needed to sign the workhouse register, which he did, stating - Name/Joseph Merrick, Date/Monday, 29th December 1879, Religion/Catholic, Birth/1861 (this was always a common error given by Joseph regarding his birthdate, records show he was born 5th August 1862). This register book with the admissions and discharges of occupants has been preserved at the Leicester Museum. Joseph was now part of the 1,180 residents in the workhouse scheme. He was handed a classification to determine his place of accommodation, this would determine which ward he was to be placed in. Joseph was classed as class one for abled male and female bodies.

The building was designed in such a way as to make it as prison-like as possible. The corridors were bare apart from the doors leading off. The walls were bare all but the red cold bricks as colour. There were storerooms, kitchens, workrooms, and labour yards, and standing at the very back was all but the bare workhouse yard which consisted of nothing but wooden benches in the dark corners of shadows formed by the overpowering building itself. The building shut out any additional light from the skies around making the area look even more dull, grey and depressing. The main constituent of the workhouse diet was supplemented porridge for breakfast, dry bread for lunch, dinner was a combination of vegetables and odd parts of meat thrown in. The workhouse broth was usually the water used for boiling the dinner. The people who stayed at these workhouses were unable to find work or were homeless, sick, widowed, elderly, mentally retarded, abandoned kids or brought to poverty by no fault of their own. All the residents were segregated into groups according to age and sex, and then sent to their separate blocks. This divided husbands from wives, children from parents, and boys from girls. Only at mealtimes, half an hour for each, were the families reunited. Joseph was placed in class one or group one which was males between the ages of sixteen to sixty, also being the group in which there was most trouble for guards and authorities with a lot of these individuals being drunks, drug takers, troublemakers, gang members, the inadequate, mentally handicapped, cripples and retards. Joseph's life was run like clockwork with the same day-by-day rituals of waking bells as early as 4.30 AM/5 AM, the hard labour of work throughout the days, tasteless meals of dry bread and slop, rest periods which were indicated and ended by bells, then at 10.30 PM dormitories were locked and gaslights extinguished signalling the end of a stressful day's work.

After only staying at the workhouse for twelve weeks Joseph decided to leave, signing himself out of the workhouse. The reasons behind this aren't well documented but Joseph later recounts when questioned, that the reason he left was because the workhouse was such hard work. He wanted once again to try and find permanent employment, but he was unsuccessful at doing this and after only four days away he returned where he stayed for the next four years. There is no knowing the difficulties or humiliations Joseph suffered whilst staying in the workhouse. He was without family or friends, it was him against the rest, in this place where his deformities attracted staff and residents. He must have suffered probably more than he would have liked to remember the taunting, ridicule, and humiliation brought on by the people around him. In later life, Joseph would talk with loathing, sorrow and horror about the time he spent at the workhouse. In 1882, when Joseph was around twenty years old, he underwent surgery on his face. The growth around his lip and mouth had grown so dramatically that it was now 22 centimetres, and it was severely affecting his speech and causing him trouble when he was eating. The operation was at the grounds of the workhouse infirmary under the direction of Dr Clement Fredrick Bryans. A large part of the mass flesh was removed. It cannot have been easy for Joseph to arrive at the decision to go through with the operation, especially in the days when life expectancy was that of only forty-five years of age, and that was for a healthy man. Joseph, by now, was frailer and the operation if not dealt with correctly could have easily led to his death, yet Joseph put his life in the hands of these professionals. The operation was only a minor success as over the course of time the mass around his mouth grew back and grew back at a rapid speed resembling that of an elephant's trunk but for the time being it had minimized his growth.

It was around this point not too long after he had recovered from his operation, aged twenty/twenty-one, that his left hip started causing him a lot more pain, making it extremely difficult for him to walk unaided and due to this he had to resort to walking with a stick for balance and support. It was also around this time, having been at the workhouse for little over four years, that he began contemplating his next move, thinking of a way out of the Poor Law scheme. This is when he first reached out to Showman and entertainer Sam Torr sending him a letter telling him of his deformities, and asking if he would be interested in hiring him for his shows as a freak act (freak shows as they were called, were very popular in those days, especially amongst the lower-class communities who would pay good money to see these strange, unique, abnormal, individuals). There have been many mistakes regarding how Joseph first became involved in the freakshows of these showmen. For a long time, it was thought that the showmen had come across Joseph and made him part of their act but in actual fact, it was Joseph who made first contact with the showman Sam Torr. Joseph explained later in life that he contacted the showman because he had heard that Sam Torr was interested in exhibiting specialities and novelties and that they then might be displayed in the theatre 'The Gaiety' and Joseph wanted a way out of the workhouse but knew employment was very unlikely so knowing his deformities attracted so much attention day by day why not try using that for employment within a freakshow and get paid for people staring and gloating at him, but unfortunately for Joseph he was unaware at how badly exploited he was about to become.

Sam Torr Facts

- Sam Torr was born in 1849, in Albion Street, Nottingham, England.
- Torr was an English music hall comedian who performed in a style known as lion comique (The *lion comique* was a type of popular entertainer in the Victorian music halls).
- He started singing in public early in life under the management of Dick Middleton, of the Atheneum, Nottingham, England.
- After a successful career in the music halls, Torr retired to Leicester, England becoming landlord of the Green Man pub in 1882.
- A year later in 1882, he took on the Gladstone Vaults in Wharf Street, converting it into a music hall - the 'Gaiety Palace' of Varieties.
- It opened on 30 April 1883, but after running into financial difficulties, closed three years later. It was during this period as a music hall promoter that Joseph wrote to Torr asking for employment as an exhibited freak.
- Sam agreed to Joseph's suggestion and set up a group of three theatrical businessmen to develop Merrick's career on the stage (Mr J Ellis, George Hitchcock, and Sam Roper).
- On 3rd August 1884, Joseph left the workhouse to start his new employment with Sam Torr.
- It was Sam Torr who decided to present Joseph as 'The Elephant Man', half man/half elephant.
- Joseph was first exhibited at the 'Gaiety Music Palace' and his first appearance was a success for the showman, Joseph wheeled in money off customers who wanted to view his unique appearance.

- Sam Torr then presented an appearance of Joseph at 'Ridge's Nottingham Music Hall'.

- They then exhibited Joseph initially around Nottingham and Joseph's hometown of Leicester, England.

- Sam Torr soon realized that he could make money exhibiting Joseph turning him into a travelling exhibit for his shows. To accomplish this the showman had to organize and secure a group of managers for Joseph. Music Hall proprietor 'J. Ellis', Travelling showman 'George Hitchcock', and Circus owner 'Sam Roper'.

- Joseph was a very good exhibitor for Sam, bringing him in a load of newer customers and earning him lots more money.

- The showman knew after only a few shows that Joseph was going to have to travel further afield because no exhibition featuring Joseph could remain for more than a week or so before the novelty of seeing him wore off.

After a handful of successful shows, on return to London for the winter period, Joseph's manager Mr. George Hitchcock (little George) decided the best option for Joseph was to go under the care of another showman who would have the skills to get him further afield and known on a bigger scale. This is when his manager got in touch with another showman entertainer, called Tom Norman who was a bigger success than Torr, so it was thought he would be able to do a better job for Joseph but sadly this was not to be. The year was late 1884 when Mr. George Hitchcock reached out to Tom Norman, the two spoke of Joseph and his career as a 'professional freak' straight away. Tom was very interested in hiring Joseph just on the descriptions George Hitchcock had told him. Only a few days went by when Tom Norman contacted Joseph's manager and told him he would take Joseph on to exhibit him in his shows as a freak. From there, the two set up a time and place where they could get together so Joseph and Tom could meet for the first time. On first meeting Joseph who was wearing his long black cloak, a black hat, and a woollen muffler concealing the greater part of his face, the first words out of Tom Norman's mouth were "God, I Can't Use You," but due to having already signed the agreements couldn't back out. Straight away the showman was very concerned that his appearance was so horrific that he might actually frighten the public so much they might have nightmares and not want to return. He commented to Mr. George Hitchcock, "If I'd have seen Joseph while he was at the Leicester workhouse, he would have never been amongst the parties to be released." Tom took Joseph on because he knew what he was doing, already being an established showman with a growing business in the entertainment of 'freak shows' which he ran in the East End of London in a shop opposite the Royal London Hospital. These 'freak shows' were a form of cheap lower-class entertainment affordable to the poorer communities and were viewed as a normal part of the culture (Freak shows were most popular from the 1820s to the 1940s which saw the organized profitable exhibition of people with physical, mental, or behavioural abnormalities).

Freak shows started long before the nineteenth century stretching back as far as the fifteen hundreds. In the sixteen hundreds there was a very popular duo of 'freaks' who were two conjoined Italian twin brothers called Lazarus Colloredo and Joannes Baptista Colloredo. They were combined at the upper body then the left leg of Joannes Baptist Colloredo stuck out of his mobile brother, Lazarus. He did not speak, kept his eyes closed and mouth open all the time, and was a parasitic twin. According to records of the Italian twins, if someone pushed the breast of Joannes Baptista, he moved his hands, ears, and lips. Records described Lazarus as courteous and handsome, unlike his brother who just dangled before him. When Lazarus was not exhibiting himself, he covered his brother with his cloak to avoid unnecessary attention. Later accounts claim that Lazarus married and had several children, none with his condition. He later was sentenced to death for killing a man but averted the execution by pointing out that this would also be killing his innocent twin brother. That was the last record of the twins, and nothing was heard of them again.

Tom Norman Facts

- Tom Norman was born Thomas Noakes on 7th May 1860, in Dallington, Sussex, England.

- He was the eldest of 17 children to Thomas Noakes, a butcher and a farmer, and his wife Eliza.

- He left school at the age of twelve to work alongside his father who taught his son his trade in return.

- After two years of working with his father, he decided to go travelling to hopefully find somewhere to settle and seek a career as a performer, he was unsuccessful in doing this and returned to London then found work as a butcher's assistant.

- Not long after working in the butcher's trade Tom Norman moved to Berkshire where he took up professional gambling. He spent all his money on this addiction and ended up penniless. So, out of options, returned yet again to London where he picked up a new addiction to heavy drinking, spending all his money on alcohol. It was around this time he began wandering the streets watching freak shows.

- Back in London, he once again took up the trade of butchering but in his free time would wander the streets and view the "novelties" at a penny gaff next to his place of employment in Islington.

- This was when he became very interested in the "freak show entertainment" business and knew with his skills he could easily do well in this trade.

- Norman realised he would be better off working alone and successfully staged his own "Electric Lady" in Hammersmith.

- At some point, he changed his birth name to Tom Norman, and renounced his inheritance. According to Joseph Merrick's biographers he stated, "Tom Norman may have changed his name to avoid shaming his family by his 'distasteful' connections to circuses and fairgrounds."

- Over the next few years Tom Norman's travelling exhibitions featured Eliza Jenkins, the "Skeleton Woman", a "Balloon Headed Baby" and a woman who bit off the heads of live rats—the "most gruesome" act Norman claimed to have seen.

- He displayed a "family of midgets" which in reality later came out to be that of two men and a borrowed baby.

- He operated a number of shops in London and Nottingham, and exhibited travelling shows throughout the country. In 1882, Norman gave a show at Islington's Royal Agricultural Hall. Unknown to Norman, the show was attended by American showman P. T. Barnum.

- Norman ran into a shortage of curiosities and travelled the country looking for new acts. He enticed human novelties into his employ with promises of generous salaries.

- In 1884, Norman came into contact with Joseph Merrick. Tom exhibited Joseph at his penny gaff shop on 123 Whitechapel Road, directly across the road from the Royal London Hospital.

At the age of twenty-one in 1884, Joseph teamed up with Tom Norman who took over the management of Joseph. Tom was an English businessman and showman specializing in displaying freaks and novelties. He operated two shops in London - one on 123 Whitechapel Road, and the other on the East India Docks Road, and exhibited travelling shows throughout the country exhibits featured a 'troupe of midgets', Eliza Jenkins, the 'Skeleton Woman', a 'Balloon Headed Baby', a 'woman who bit off the heads of live rats', 'the world's tallest man who was around 7ft', the 'worlds ugliest woman', a 'fat lady', the 'girl with four legs', 'John chambers known as the armless carpenter', 'retired white seamen painted black and speaking in an invented language', and now 'Joseph Merrick'. Joseph's first appearance was in the shop on Whitechapel Road, London, this was towards the end of November 1884, his job was a professional freak. Joseph was positioned at the back of the shop, just in front of him hung a large canvas sheet so he wouldn't frighten passersby. This sheet was painted with the terrifying image of a man halfway through the process of turning into an elephant, this was first shown by Tom to customers with him announcing "Ladies and gentlemen, I ask you please prepare yourselves – brace yourself up to witness one who is probably the most horrendous human beings to ever breathe the air of life - let me introduce you to the Elephant Man." For customers to witness this they first had to pay the two-pence entry fee. When the sheet was drawn back and people saw Joseph for the first time, the crowd gasped in horror, some people screamed, some fainted, some cried, some shouted that he was the creation of the devil himself, others would spit at Joseph calling him all sorts of names, this was completely expectable to Tom who would only intervene if customers attempted to attack Joseph physically, he did this not out of love or protection towards Joseph but because he knew Joseph was too much of an aspect to him and didn't want to jeopardize Joseph being hurt, and then unable to work for him. Between shows Tom was very unkind to Joseph, beating him if he was unable to make the earnings expected of him (in retrospect these beatings were unnecessary as it wasn't due to lack of trying on Joseph's behalf but in fact, it was bad sale skills by Tom Norman, with him not being able to coerce the general public to buy tickets for his shows which resulted in no earnings, so it was nothing more than a desperate, bitter man unhappy with his lack of earnings by no one's fault but his own and taking his anger out on someone vulnerable, unable to defend themselves). Tom drank heavily and was by all accounts an alcoholic who put drink before everything, he would drink the equivalent of up to two or three bottles of vodka a day and some days he'd drink until he passed out, he smoked heavily too so this would have definitely made him a very unpleasant man to be around. Tom was known to be violent once he'd had a drink which was every day and known to take his anger out on others. Probably Joseph was the go-to for his outbursts as Joseph was a gentle soul who would never fight back. On the rare occasions he was in good spirits he could be seen being nice to his "novities". It was Tom who first witnessed the odd position Joseph slept. One morning as Tom woke he walked past Joseph's dull-lit room and in between the curtains could see he was sleeping sitting upright with his legs drawn upwards, and his head resting on his knees. Joseph later explained he had had to sleep this way since he was in his mid-teens because his head had become so misshaped and heavy that lying down would either cause him to choke (due to his air supply being cut off) or the risk of waking up with a broken neck. The showman did attempt to try and find a solution for Joseph's sleeping difficulties with the help of one of his friends who was a carpenter - a man called Joe Wintle. He attempted to create a type of structure that would allow Joseph to sleep lying down, it was a basketwork frame, padded with lambswool, which could be strapped to Joseph's shoulders allowing him to lie down but they could never get it where it was a comfortable position for Joseph so the idea was scrapped and that was the last time Tom was known to have shown Joseph any affection or sympathy. Between shows, Joseph wasn't allowed out for his own protection from the general public. When he was assorted out into the streets, he was always to wear his long black cloak, black hat, and the woollen muffler concealing the greater part of his face. This was to prevent frightening the public and also to keep him hidden away, so if people were interested in seeing Joseph they would have to pay the two-pence entry fee at Norman's "Penny Gaff shop". Only a few weeks after Joseph had teamed up with Tom Norman, when he was aged twenty-two, police closed down the show (it was around this period people started viewing the "abnormal freaks" more as humans and individuals rather than the deformed cripples sprung by the devil they were known as). Luckily for Joseph within these few weeks of the show being opened a steady stream of students from the Royal London Hospital directly across the road on 123 Whitechapel were beginning to visit the shop on their lunch breaks out of curiosity about what was inside, having heard about the so-called "freaks" hid indoors. It was during one of these visits from students that a young surgeon in training called Dr Tuckett introduced himself to the manager of Joseph, Tom Norman and asked if he could have a private meeting with the "Elephant Man" he had been hearing about. The two of them chatted for a while and finally settled on a price for a private viewing. After the doctor had witnessed the sighting of

Joseph he was so taken aback out of disbelief by his many deformities that he asked if it would be okay if one of his colleagues, a Mr. Fredrick Treves might be granted the same privilege, to which the showman promptly said yes. The very next day Tom was in a nearby coffee shop ordering breakfast for himself when a Surgeon who worked at the Royal London Hospital on Whitechapel Road called Fredrick Treves was introduced to Tom by the student he had chatted to only the day before. They walked back to the shop together whilst Fredrick asked many questions to the showman about his history working with "novities" and his fascination with freak shows. Once back at the shop, the showman treated Mr. Treves to a quick run-through of the normal routines of the day but allowed no longer than a quarter of an hour. As soon as the time was up he insisted, "I must get back to my breakfast, please leave." Later that day Dr Treves sent Dr Tuckett back across the road to the shop to negotiate with Tom Norman about bringing Joseph to the hospital to be examined, Joseph himself raised no objection to this request whilst the showman saw it as "advantage of publicity", so he agreed.

Joseph visited the hospital two or three times within the following weeks, the first being in December 1884, after Dr Tuckett negotiated to bring him over to be studied and explained the manner in which they wished to use Joseph for future understandings of his disease. When Joseph first arrived, he had to stay in the waiting area until Dr Treves was ready to see him. The members of staff on the ward of the waiting area were shocked by his deformities and sickened by the foul smell coming from him. When Fredrick was ready he came and escorted Joseph to his office and began conducting small tasks for Joseph to undertake so he could understand his abilities and brain functionality (strangely in the whole relationship between Dr Fredrick Treves and Joseph he always had his name incorrect and called Joseph 'John' whether this was because Fredrick misheard Joseph at the time of asking his name or if he had misheard Dr Tuckett's description at the beginning of the discussion has never been made very clear but this is the case and Fredrick always presented Joseph and told people his name was John – Joseph never corrected this error with Dr Treves). After he had assessed Joseph, the next stage on his next visit was that Fredrick would present Joseph to the Pathological Society of London where he was going to discuss Joseph's abnormalities amongst other professions, and then try to come up with some explanation to understand Joseph's disfigurements. The examination went as follows: his head measured 36 inches in circumference, his right hand was 12 inches in circumference at the wrist, his whole body (except his genitals) was covered with tumours, his legs and left hip were so deformed he had to walk with a cane, over the course of time Joseph's abnormal skin and bone growth had done much damage to his body, the giant skin folds had made his head so abnormally heavy that he was forced to sleep sitting upright in a chair but otherwise underneath all the physical abnormalities he was found to be in good health. Unfortunately for Joseph, in doing this he had to be depicted naked in front of a room of professionals all studying him intensely, which for Joseph was very uncomfortable and embarrassing. After being observed, treated like an animal, prodded, and pointed at by loads of unfamiliar faces, Joseph decided he did not want to continue going to the hospital because, in his own words, "it made me feel unhuman". In his own words, he said regarding the matter, "I do not mind being displayed discreetly and decently when I am being paid, but over at the hospital I was stripped naked and made to feel like an animal in a cattle market." A few weeks passed before the next request was sent from Treves to examine Joseph further, but this time the manager Tom turned it down, Fredrick was outraged by the dismissal from the showman because his objective was not to make Joseph feel the way he did and in fact, he was only trying to help him but before he could help Joseph he had to determine and understand Joseph's disorder. He wrote in his book titled 'The Elephant Man and Other Reminiscences' released in 1923, "Looking back I know I handled the situation incorrectly and should have been more understanding to the feelings of Joseph Merrick, I tried desperately to get him back onto the ward of the hospital so I could help and study him further but unfortunately he wasn't interested, it was only out of utter despair on Joseph's behalf that our paths met again."

When the police closed down the "freak show shop" on Whitechapel Road, London in early 1885, it was never made definite if it was

Fredrick who laid a complaint against the exhibition, or if they were responding to a shift in public opinion demanding a tightening up of the standards of what was considered fit for public viewing. The forces of responsibility were making a determined-on-slaughter attack with these viewings of abnormal, deformed human beings to be seen as distasteful and wrong. By 1885, a distaste for 'freak shows' had developed in Britain and Joseph along with his manager George Hitchcock decided to move the Elephant Man exhibit, so they decided to tour Europe. Joseph travelled alongside his other manager Sam Roper. According to a verbal tradition he was allowed during his time with the circus his own small caravan to travel in and enjoy a degree of privacy. Along on their journey with them were two young men known as 'Roper's midgets'. Their actual names were Dooley and Harry Bramley, who were brothers. They were amateur boxers in their spare time. The two men were very kind and patient with Joseph and would happily stand guard to ward off any unwelcome attention Joseph might attract. Dooley himself would make a point of visiting Joseph in his caravan when they were having quiet periods to make sure he was happy and well within himself. They both would sit and chat for hours. He stated, "I was impressed by Joseph's standard of conversations, a most interesting man – he would talk about topics that you would never really think a man in his condition would talk about – he was a bit on the religious side too." The brothers recalled a time when Joseph found himself in a difficult situation being harassed by a group of hooligans, the ringleader took hold of Joseph's cloak to try to pull it off him, but the brothers came to his defence and scared off the bullies with their boxing skills and abilities to throw good punches. The shows themselves met with only mediocre success because it was becoming clear that no matter how often they moved around Europe they were now met with a lot of anger and distaste for the novities freak shows which for the times was a good step in the right direction, but for people like Joseph or the other abnormal humans who participated in these freak shows it was far from good, for the showmen knew only of this trade and without it they would be out of a job. After trying and failing to make a name for himself in Europe, and now out of options, once they arrived in Belgium in a large, populated city called Brussels, Joseph's manager Sam Roper with the help of Tom Norman beat him, robbing him of his life savings (£55.00) which Joseph had saved up from working in the 'Penny Gaff Shop', abandoned him, leaving him lost, alone and penniless, in a city where he had neither friends nor hope of assistance and where he was unable to communicate with those around him. Joseph never saw his circus managers again (£55.00 in the late nineteen hundreds was worth roughly £5,200.00 in today's money).

It was now 1886, Joseph was around age twenty-four.

Joseph struggled to find his feet and was sadly homeless yet again, only this time for a longer stretch. Nearly a year went by with Joseph being homeless, having to fend for himself and begging on the streets but over this year of homelessness, he managed to save up enough money to board a boat back to England. To make this money he did have to beg and pawn what little he had. As he attempted to board the ferry for Dover he was refused passage because the crew member of the ferry was worried that Joseph would frighten the other passengers. So he had to travel to Antwerp and from there was able to board a ship to Harwich in Essex and then onwards to Liverpool Street, London, but this travelled around the way of Rotterdam, a long way to the north and an overall longer and more expensive journey. On his journey back to London he was met with faces of strangers who spoke in languages he couldn't understand, pressing against the carriage windows in an attempt to catch a glimpse beneath the hat's vail covering his face, if he descended from the train, the crowds mercilessly followed his bizarre, shuffling figure until he was forced to hide away. On his return, he also contracted a 'bronchial infection' (Bronchitis is an infection of the lungs causing them to become inflamed and irritated, similar to what his mother suffered with and later died of). He finally travelled by train to London and arrived at Liverpool Street station. After he arrived at the platform on Liverpool Street Station he needed assistance but was met with strangers running in horror as Joseph approached them or had them make no attempt to understand his broken speech. There were no hotel or lodging houses that would allow him accommodation, no café or restaurants that would serve him, and no hospitals that would accept him as a patient (he couldn't share a public ward or afford to pay for a private one). The attention his figure drew was instant, whether he tried to move away or stand still the crowds would gather around him with murmuring comments, finger-pointing, and stares. He was then harassed by a gang of hooligans who began following Joseph, calling him names. One of them attempted to pull off his face covering and hat but was unsuccessful, then another attempted to trip Joseph trying to make him fall, yet again unsuccessful, but this frightened Joseph causing him to try run away. This only drew more attention to him and he was then mobbed by a big group of people who began to chase him. Joseph managed to outrun them for a short while until they managed to corner him, he was now surrounded by 15-20 people who were all hurling insults at him and calling him horrible names, it was at this point Joseph ran out of energy, collapsing to the floor and began crying making sounds of distress and panic, repeating over, "Please I am a human being - just leave me be." All this uproar caught the attention of the security staff at the station and the patrolling police officers who quickly intervened and took Joseph to safety in the staff room. Joseph then closed up, collapsed to the floor, huddled into a ball and began crying. After Joseph had been offered a glass of water and had calmed down enough from the traumatic experience he had just faced, they attempted to talk to Joseph but unable to understand his shaken voice they searched him for any form of identification. They didn't find any, but they did eventually find a Dr Frederick Treves's business card in a pocket and contacted him. His day of work at the hospital must have barely started on the morning of 24th June 1886, when the message arrived at his desk asking him to go assist the staff and police at Liverpool station. When he arrived at the station the crowd was still gathered with people scattered about the platform. Fredrick had to push his way through the crowd just to get to the waiting room where Joseph was being held. Fredrick instantly recognised the figure huddled close against the wall wrapped up into a tight ball as that of Joseph Merrick. He looked as if he was trying to shrink away causing the illusion that he was non-existent. Fredrick realized that Joseph was now beyond the limits of human endurance and was utterly broken.

After explaining the situation and who he was to Joseph, the surgeon agreed to take responsibility and accompanied a frightened, shaken-up Joseph back to the London hospital with the assistance of the London police who helped get Joseph away from the crowd and into a cab. Joseph questioned nothing but sat in a silent daze as if overcome with a trusting sense of calm. Then as the cab pulled out of the train station Joseph sagged into a sudden childlike sleep of calmness. On the drive back to the hospital with Joseph having a well-needed sleep Fredrick couldn't get over the foul smell from his relaxed body. Fredrick later stated in his book 'The Elephant Man and Other Reminiscences', "the smell was baring such a bad stench lingering on his body that it could make eyes water and the toughest of stomachs gip with the feeling of sick, it was here I began to consider the implications of the responsibilities I had taken on." Fredrick was undoubtedly an angel sent to the broken Joseph, if it wasn't for him to come to Joseph's rescue on that early morning of June, the police would have probably sent Joseph to be shut away somewhere in an anonymous institution to await his death. When the cab pulled up to the London Hospital, Joseph was helped to a small single-bedded, isolated ward tucked away up in the attic. Here he soaked in a well-needed bath, was assisted with washing his body, given a well-needed meal, then put to bed to sleep and rebuild his strength.

Over the next coming days, Fredrick examined Joseph at the hospital and found that his condition had severely deteriorated in the previous two years since he was last in the care of the hospital. When Fredrick had last carried out his examinations two years prior, it was the surgeon's assumption that Joseph was incurable at the time, he also deemed Joseph unattached of emotions and feelings due to the fact his facial deformities prevented him from forming any expressions. Only by the use of words was he able to express how he was feeling but because his speech was so impaired and distorted beyond comprehension, his intelligence and awareness of things happening around him tended to go unrecognised. In the early days when he first arrived at the hospital, Fredrick put forward some difficult questions to Joseph, asking him about his past but mainly about his childhood and growing up. This was a very difficult time for Joseph to relive even in memory, so he would only give brief answers to the questions given such as 'it was a nightmare', 'I hated living at home', 'I was treated as an outcast.' He gave Fredrick the impression that he knew nothing about his father or sibling, which in retrospect he didn't really. After avoiding home life for many years when his mother died, along with not wanting to go home to his distant, emotionless father and a stepmother who never showed him any signs of affection or warmth, then leaving home when he was only seventeen, it's a fair assumption to say Joseph probably knew very little about his father and sibling growing up and what he could remember were not fond memories so he probably subconsciously blocked it all out, which is why Fredrick got the impression he knew very little about his father. After a peaceful couple of months of Joseph being able to regain his strength and having the privacy that he very much loved, it was now time for Dr Treves and other staff at the hospital to attempt to find Joseph a more suitable place for him to live with the benefit of that facility being able to provide Joseph with the care he needed. The London Hospital on Whitechapel Road was considered incapable of caring for "incurables" such as Joseph, so it seemed when he had regained his strength Joseph would have to find other accommodation away from the London Hospital as they were out of options on how they could help, but luckily, he was being given the assistance from the staff to locate an ideal place for him that he would be happy with, which for Joseph was all but bittersweet.

Fredrick Treves Facts

- Frederick Treves was born on 15th February 1853, in Dorset, in the town of Dorchester, England.

- As a small boy at the age of seven, he attended the small Dorchester school which his brothers attended before him, it was run by the Dorset dialect poet William Barnes headmaster (William Barnes born 22nd February 1801 was an English polymath, writer, poet, philologist, priest, mathematician, engraving artist and inventor. He died on 7th October 1886).

- Fredrick only stayed at William Barnes School for two years.

- He was known to be a very timid, shy boy who would, the moment lessons were over, run to hide in the cloakroom behind the coats of other students until the family maid came to assort him home.

- When he was eleven he attended the "Merchant Taylors' School" (a selective British independent public school for boys founded in 1561 in London).

- He stayed at the Merchant Taylors' School until he was eighteen, but as an intelligent young man with what seemed the signs of a bright future ahead of him, he left with an undistinguished record.

- It was soon decided by his parents that he should follow in the footsteps of his eldest brother, who had been a medical student at St Thomas's Hospital.

- Though London Hospital was a place of medical schooling it was only one of many at the time in London and in young Fredrick's mind it was one of the least appealing to him and was considered to be generally one of the least attractive to students because of its location.

- London Hospital itself could claim to be the largest in England, but it was set in the midst of the largest and poorest population in the country. Its 690 beds were mainly occupied by patients from a maze of alleys and back streets that ran behind the river of the docks of the lower Thames in London's west end (Most commonly known in 1888 as the area that serial killer, "Jack the Ripper" stalked, killed, and decapitated his victims in, leaving them dead on the streets of London near and around the East and West end).

- Fredrick attended 'The London Hospital Medical College' (commonly known as Barts, a medical and dental school in London. The school is part of Queen Mary University of London.)

- The busy, robust atmosphere at the London Hospital seemed to suit Fredrick who began to achieve greatly at tasks he undertook and displayed a practical approach to the problems he encountered.

- He passed the membership examinations for the Royal College of Surgeons of England in 1875, and in 1878 for the fellowship of the Royal College of Surgeons.

- Fredrick began his medical career as a General Practitioner, becoming a partner in a medical practice in Wirksworth, Derbyshire, England.

- Due to his strong personality, intelligence in the medical profession and overall confidence he portrayed, he wasn't looked on highly by his work peers who were becoming jealous and envious of the young, ambitious doctor.

- Due to the jealous atmosphere at work and having met a woman whom he would later marry, he moved away from the area of Derbyshire to London where he became a surgeon, specialising in abdominal surgery, at the London Hospital in the late nineteenth century.

- In 1884, Dr Fedrick Treves first met Joseph whom he brought to the London Hospital where Joseph stayed.

- After Joseph Merrick died, Fredrick created a memorandum about Joseph and his first encounter with him, he stated, "On my first encounter with John (Joseph) there stood revealed the most disgusting beast of humanity that I had ever seen, in the course of my professional career I'd come across many deformities but at no one time had I met such a degraded or perverted virgin of a human being as this lone figure displayed in front of me."

- Although this remark first made by Fredrick sounds ruthless and cruel, he later went on to be arguably one of Joseph's closest friends. That in itself says a lot about a person's personality as like everyone else when Fredrick first met Joseph, he too was shocked by his appearance but as their friendship developed, he realised his appearance was part of him, but definitely didn't define him in any way.

⊷⊷⊰⊲⟨⟩⊳⊶⊷

Later Life 1886-1889

The arrangement Fredrick had set up for Joseph with the ward in the attic although nothing special, for Joseph it must have felt like a whole new world of freedom and peace. It gave Joseph a roof over his head and the privacy he loved, Fredrick arranged everything for him to make the ward feel homely and look the way Joseph wanted it to. For the first two to three weeks Joseph remained unsettled and apprehensive but when the routine of structured hospital life, with nurse visits to his room played out Joseph began to settle. Fredrick arranged it so members of staff would check in on Joseph a few times a day and bring him meals and other beverages. He did however have to hire additional staff to tend to Joseph because a lot of the staff at the hospital were too afraid to go into his room as his appearance frightened them, new staff were briefed on Joseph's appearance beforehand and then showed pictures of his deformities, so they knew what to expect. Unfortunately for some, this wasn't enough and once they encountered Joseph in person they refused to look after him. Over the course of the next few weeks unable to get any extra staff to assist with helping Joseph, the staff already working at the hospital began to slowly pull together and take food up to Joseph and slowly began to assist him with whatever he needed help with (Usually, these were only minor tasks, puffing his pillows, opening/closing windows, passing him items of his possessions). It was on these occasions that staff slowly started to realise that Joseph, apart from his appearance, was not any different after all and in fact, was like everybody else. They were able to chat with him about many topics. Even though at times they found it difficult to understand Joseph they all began to warm up to his kind, humble nature. Joseph began to form good friendships with the hospital staff and surgeons, he was always very timid and shy around them but appreciated everything the staff did for him. A lot of the time he was unable to articulate his appreciation to the staff due to his fragile, broken voice so he would assemble many complex, cardboard cut-out model kits, drawing the fine details within the structures or neatly coloured in them, then presenting these to the staff as gifts of appreciation he enjoyed assembling these cut-outs so much he began decorating them around his room (There is a remaining cardboard cut-out which Joseph assembled that is preserved at the London museum). Fredrick would visit Joseph daily, sometimes more than once, as time went on he became incredibly accustomed to Joseph's speech and found a greater understanding of his speech difficulties, this meant he was able to talk with Joseph and study him more easily. Though at first it was nothing more than a doctor/patient relationship, over time the relationship blossomed, and they became closer, with Fredrick staying and talking to Joseph one-on-one for long periods. He became impressed at how intelligent and insightful Joseph was. He states in his book 'The Elephant Man and Other Reminiscences', "John (Joseph) was a very intelligent man who loved to read, only after a couple of months living on the hospital ward, he had devoured his way through a large quantity of books. Along with reading, he was a fine artist who loved to paint and create tremendous life-like building structures and display them around his room." By November 1886, Joseph now aged towards the end of twenty-five. Five months had gone by since he was first admitted to the ward and while he could definitely not be described as physically fit or healthy, there was little more improvement that could have been achieved with Joseph or with the treatments the hospital had to offer. Unknown to Joseph, Fredrick and the chairman of the London Hospital, Carr Gromm, were attempting to find another hospital for Joseph to stay where they would be able to offer him the help and support he desperately needed but once they explained the complex needs of Joseph all the hospitals refused to take him on as a patient. Whether this was because they didn't have the knowledge or skillsets needed to match Joseph, or if they didn't have the space for such a disfigured man with such complex needs, or if they simply didn't want to take him on because they along with many other hospitals thought his appearance would frighten and upset the other patients is all unknown, but sadly for Joseph, he was out of luck once again, with no other hospitals or facilities willing to help him. After trying and failing to find another hospital which would accommodate Joseph, plus not wanting to let him go, knowing he would only become homeless once again, the hospital staff were out of options. There were no funds available to maintain Joseph in the hospital ward permanently. After discussing with Fredrick what they should do next, the chairman of the London Hospital, Carr Gromm, decided to publish a letter in 1887, with the 'The Times Newspaper' describing Joseph's case and asking for help from whoever was willing, it read as followed,

"I am authorised to ask your powerful assistance in bringing to the notice of the public the following most exceptional case. There is a little room off one of our attic wards with a man named Joseph Merrick, aged about twenty-five, a native of Leicester, so dreadful a sight that he isn't even able to come out by daytime for fear of shocking and horrifying others. He has been called the 'Elephant Man' on account of his terrible deformities. I will not shock your readers with any detailed descriptions of his infirmities, but only one arm has the look of a normal body part and is available for work."

In the letter, Carr Gomm also outlined Joseph's history within the Poor Law, workhouse scheme, how he was exhibited in freak shows, and how he travelled to Belgium only to be beaten, robbed, and abandoned in a city. He didn't know then how he pawned his last possessions to allow him to raise his fare back to England. Mr Carr Gomm then explained in detail the mighty difficulties Joseph's case raised but that he ought to be treated with the greatness of kindness because sorrow and misery were all he had ever known. Not long after, a publicity campaign was set in motion on Joseph's behalf though it is unclear who set it up. Nevertheless, the outcome from the public and kindness towards Joseph was astonishing and letters started appearing daily to the hospital. Donations started pouring in to help this strange individual people had read about. Letters were arriving day by day with considerable sums of money, £50 here, £100 there. About £150 had been sent by a Mr Singer who had offered a contribution of £50 yearly donation for Joseph to be kept there on the hospital wards indefinitely. A huge sum of £240 had been sent for

Joseph by his Uncle Charles, who along with the donation attached a letter sending his love and wishes to his nephew (although he would never see his nephew again). This letter, released to the public, resulted in a sympathetic public outpour of donations and eventually enough financial donations provided Joseph with a permanent home on a ward at the hospital where several rooms in the London Hospital were converted into living quarters for him at the back of the building. Joseph had not long turned twenty-six when it was first explained to him that there were going to be renovations made at the hospital to his benefit with the donation money raised so he could stay and live permanently. He did not understand why this was being done, it had to be explained to him three different times because he couldn't understand the generosity of everybody. Staff at the hospital put on a tiny party for Joseph to congratulate him on his new home. Present that day were all the staff he had become so fond of and who had in return become so fond of him. They congratulated him by buying him moving-in presents they thought he would appreciate. He was ecstatic, completely overjoyed and in disbelief at the generosity of the public who raised the donations for him and to the staff for the gifts. He gave a little speech where he gracefully thanked everyone for everything, they had done for him over the last few months, saying how kind and lovely they all were. It was met with cheers and praises for Joseph. Joseph then began to cry with tears of happiness. Now that Joseph was finally for the first time in his life settled in a homely environment where he was happy, he was able to enjoy the remaining years of his life doing whatever made him most happy. The thing he enjoyed doing most was constructing the cardboard cut-out kits he had become so accustomed to while being in the hospital ward. He could spend hours in the day assembling these. He could be found late at night wandering the halls of his living quarters, he loved walking in the hospital gardens although he was only able to do this on occasions when it was quiet. This is probably why he chose to do his wandering in the night knowing the majority of patients would be asleep (Joseph always slept in until midday then he was known to be up into the early morning hours. Whether or not he preferred the nights to days, which, because he slept away his mornings does seem to suggest that, will only ever have been truly known to Joseph himself. Did he feel more comfortable with the dark nights making it less likely anybody would see him, we will never know for certain). His main interest was reading. He enjoyed reading anything he could get his hands on, this could be newspapers or magazines of all kinds. In fact, he was known to read any scrap of writing that fell into his hands. Joseph loved books more about the romantic aspect of life, he loved the play 'Romeo and Juliet'. Joseph was an excellent writer and over his time at the hospital, his love of writing blossomed. He found that writing gave him a sense of comfort in a life that had been so tragic. He also loved writing letters and poetry. He was known on occasion for writing his own short poems. These were always romance-based. After all the heartache, misery, and abuse – mentally, physically, and emotionally that Joseph had endured for the main percentage of his life, you would think he would have a very negative, pessimistic opinion of humans but in actual fact, it was the complete opposite. Joseph actually thought very highly of people and understood that the majority of individuals were kind and loving. He had been unlucky with a lot of the people he had come in contact with. He thought very fondly of the opposite sex and placed women on almost a pedestal, for in his opinion they were beautiful beings inside and out (Joseph had only ever known one woman which was his mother whom he truly adored and placed on a pedestal. It is possible because Joseph had only ever known her love that he just assumed every other woman must be the same - a very naive yet heartwarming assumption).

Fredrick and Joseph spoke many times about women and the fact Fredrick was married with children fascinated Joseph. He would ask loads of questions about what it was like being a father, what it felt like to be in love and to be loved by another, what it was like to hold a lady's hand and so on. Fredrick realised that Joseph's image of the opposite sex was very intense and his attitude towards women could be defined in the simplest of terms: he felt an admiration towards them, they were people with such an awe about them that they should not be approached let alone, in Joseph's mind, obtainable. Joseph's imagination of a woman was they were and should be as they existed in the pages of the romantic novels - delicate, more finely moulded creatures than men, who needed to be protected, cherished and above all worshipped. Unknown to Joseph and the staff who cared for him, it was coming up to the last two years of Joseph's life, it was now early 1889 with Joseph having just turned twenty-six.

There were occasions when Fredrick found himself peering in on Joseph only to find that he looked bored, lonely and unhappy within himself. He was worried the rooms in the back of the hospital where Joseph stayed were becoming a prison. Joseph's isolation from people around him like before was happening again, only this time Fredrick felt it was his fault and he was to blame. However, Fredrick felt for certain that much of Joseph's distress sprung from the loneliness life had unfortunately forced on him. To Fredrick, it seemed that these sufferings came in part from having been rejected by so many fellow human beings. It was because of this reason he thought it may be a good idea to let Joseph get out and about more regardless of what others thought of him. Joseph had spent a huge part of his life hidden away and since he was getting older, Fredrick knew he didn't have much longer and wanted to make the remaining of his life something which he could enjoy. He started by taking him out one-on-one up to the countryside where they could look at all the greenery and mountains together. Joseph was in his element, completely in awe of the sights he was seeing, he had never been to the county before so for him it would have been absolutely astonishing. It was already common knowledge to the staff at the London Hospital that Joseph loved anything nature-based, so this must have been something incredible for Joseph to have witnessed. Fredrick next arranged for Joseph to visit his home address where he lived with his wife and children, then to stay for a meal with them (His children weren't present as Fredrick, in the end, was concerned they would be too scared seeing Joseph in person). When Joseph was told of this event he was excited like a little kid at Christmas. He had never before been in a loving family home decorated with pictures and ornaments. So he looked forward to this for the whole week leading up to it, discussing his excitement amongst staff who came to assist him on their daily routines. The staff in return listened to Joseph and joined in with his excitement, expressing, "You're going to have a lovely time." On the afternoon of the arranged activity, Joseph was assisted with washing himself and helped with putting on a suit he wanted to wear for the meal. For the first time in his life, he felt proud and looked smart, with the female members of staff commenting, "You looked very handsome." This comment would for the average person have meant nothing compared to what it did to Joseph. He states later on to Fredrick in one of their one-on-one conversations that it was the first time in his entire life a female had called him handsome, and it meant the world to him giving him so much pride and joy, completely boosting up his confidence. (It's these small gestures of human kindness that mean so much to individuals such as Joseph, not that in any way he thinks of himself as handsome or anything of the sort but with it being just a nice comment to make towards somebody like Joseph, which he will appreciate beyond comprehension and give him some self-confidence he most definitely deserves.) When they arrived at the home of Fredrick and his wife, on Coldwell Street in London, they were greeted by Fredrick's wife who kindly invited them in. Fredrick first showed Joseph around the house whilst his wife finished making the food. Fredrick later states, "Our house was only small and had very little ornaments or items of interest on display, and at first I was a little embarrassed showing Joseph the house as I wanted to show him some almighty, grand property which our house was most definitely not but in spite of this, it took forever to look around the house because Joseph was showing an incredible interest in every aspect of the house, every cushion, curtain, wallpaper, admiring the pictures wanting to know who each person in the photo was, finding the artwork and ornaments fascinating, wanting to know who painted them or where they came from, he was even fascinated with the furniture asking what it was like to own such a beautiful piece of luxury in their home." After touring the house they were invited into the dining room for food. There is no information about the actual mealtime itself, but we know Joseph came away from the house extremely happy and content so it all must have been good. One can only imagine what the topics of conversation might have been, more likely being topics of where he grew up, what things was he interested in, has he got a big family, etc. Joseph, on the other hand, being the thoughtful soul he was, probably asked questions related to them and their family steering the conversation away from himself.

Next, Fredrick thought it might be very beneficial for Joseph if he could meet people who would disregard his appearance and actually treat and talk to him as a normal human being, unlike the lifetime he has spent of individuals sniggering, mocking, and humiliating him. He asked a female friend of his who was young, pretty, and recently widowed if she would be up to the task. From being her friend Fredrick knew she was genuine and would talk to Joseph respectfully, completely putting his appearance aside and treating him the way he deserved. She was a lady called Mrs Leila Maturin, who had lost her husband, Dr Leslie Maturin, in 1883, having only been married for approximately two months. Fredrick insisted that when she was to visit Joseph she could knock on his door and enter with a smile, wish him good morning, and shake his hand. He went on to explain it was crucial that she show no signs of shock or embarrassment. Without hesitation, Mrs Maturin accepted Fredrick's request, and then Fredrick accompanied Leila Maturin to Joseph's living quarters to meet him. She entered the room gracefully just as she had been informed to do, smiling as she approached, reaching out and shaking Joseph's hand while greeting him with a "good morning", "I hope you are well". Unfortunately, it was all too much for Joseph, words were beyond him, slowly he released her hand bowed his head in silence and broke down into a harrowing sob and wept uncontrollably. Later that day Joseph confided to Fredrick that it was in fact the first time any woman had smiled at him, let alone take his hand in greeting. This was a shock to Fredrick who could barely believe what he was hearing, that Joseph was so neglected of friendly attention that he broke down but it gave Fredrick a good idea. With the public campaign set up on Joseph's behalf, it resulted in him being valued by members of the British upper class who wanted to help him. So Fredrick thought due to this why not have members of the public who so kindly donated on Joseph's behalf be able to meet, sit down and chat with him, as long as Joseph agreed that was.

After weeks of planning and building up Joseph's confidence, people began entering his room to have pleasantry talks with Joseph. At first, he was reserved towards his guests, but every introduction seemed to bring him more confidence and each day his personality blossomed more, and he began to talk freely, completely oblivious of his speech difficulties. Dr Treves still had to be present as the interpreter, but over time this did help improve his speaking, although it was only a very minor improvement. Eventually, this was a huge success and individuals who wanted to help Joseph all started showing up at the hospital to greet and talk to him. They would do as instructed, enter with a smile, offer a hand for greeting, exchange pleasantries, sit down and talk to Joseph one-on-one. Over time many of these people formed friendships with Joseph and would come back to see him time and time again. This was a big boost to Joseph and his confidence. For the first time, he began to form his own personality which everyone loved. Later, after he died, a lot of his friends came out and spoke of Joseph saying, "He was such a gentle, kind, man, so humble in his ways without an ounce of hatred, a loyal man who enjoyed nothing more than putting a smile on your face." Along with the general public's interest in Joseph, the letter put out by Carr Gromm, chairman of London Hospital, also attracted the attention of people who were in positions to bring social influences on his behalf. He received visits from the wealthy ladies and gentlemen of London society. This included surgeon John Bland-Sutton, other well-known surgeons and doctors of the time, but most notably Alexandra, Princess of Wales and actress, Mrs Kendal to whom her husband was the actor W. H. Kendal.

Madge Kendal Facts

- Dame Madge Kendal was born Margaret Shafto Robertson on 15th March 1848.

- She was born in Grimsby in Lincolnshire, England, where her father ran a chain of theatres.

- Her father was from a theatrical family. He performed at eight theatres which his family owned in towns in and around Lincolnshire and later became manager of some of these.

- Her mother was from a Dutch family and her father (Madge's grandfather) taught languages in London, so she spoke English with no trace of a foreign accent which Madge would later pick up and adapt too.

- Madge began to act as a small child, making her London debut at the age of four. As a teenager, she appeared with 'Ellen' and 'Kate Terry' in 'Bath', and played Shakespeare's 'Ophelia and Desdemona' in the West End.

- In 1855, Madge played 'Eva' in a dramatized *'Uncle Tom's Cabin'*, in which she had four songs. Her singing was much praised, and an operatic career seemed possible, but she contracted diphtheria, and her voice suffered after the removal of her tonsils.

- Under the management of 'J. B. Buckstone', she joined the company of the 'Haymarket Theatre' in London in 1869, when she was 21.

- While in the company she met and married the actor 'W. H. Kendal'. After their marriage, in August 1869, the two made it a rule to appear in the same productions and became known to the public as 'The Kendals'.

- After a series of generally successful appearances in London and on tour in Britain, the Kendals joined the actor 'John Hare' in running the 'St James's Theatre' between 1879 and 1889, transforming the fortunes of their theatre, previously known for financial failure.

- For the first time, the theatre's reputation was steadily defied. The new owners aimed both to amuse and to improve public taste.

- Under their management, St James's staged twenty-one plays, seven were new British pieces, eight adaptations of French plays, and the rest were revivals.

- The Kendals, partially Madge herself, became associated in the public mind with the transformation of the theatrical profession from disreputable to respectable.

- The Kendals imposed a high moral code on the members of their company both on stage and behind the scenes. Another commentator wrote, "Mrs Kendal, one of the best artists of her sex on the London stage, is in private life the epitome of all domestic virtues and graces." She was dubbed the 'Matron of the English Theatre'.

- Madge was generally considered a finer actor than her husband and was particularly known for her performances in comic parts.

- All her life she never shied away from performing generous acts of charity work.

- It was because of this kind nature of hers that she was able to come across Joseph in 1888.

- The two formed a good friendship with them both sending gifts back and forth to each other.

- She and her husband were known to visit Joseph on many occasions up in his living quarters at the hospital.

- She helped raise funds and public sympathy for Joseph.

- After the friendship blossomed between the two, she invited Joseph to watch her perform at the 'St James's Theatre'.

Final Year-1890

At the time in the late 1880s, and early 1890s, Madge Kendal was performing at the St James's Theatre in Piccadilly, Manchester, alongside her husband's business partner in theatrical management, Mr John Hare. The pair worked extremely well with each other, whatever they appeared in together they excelled at, this made Mrs Kendal, in particular, a star performer with a huge following. In her whole life, Madge never shied away from charity work or helping those less fortunate, this is how she came across Joseph, when a friend in the entertainment business told Mrs Kendal of this deformed figure known as the 'elephant man'. It has not been made clear exactly when she first met Joseph but nonetheless, at some point, she did arrange a meeting with the help of Fredrick Treves. On first meeting Joseph she wasn't worried about the encounter, in fact, she was calm and well-spoken doing exactly as she was told by Fredrick. On the first arrival, she instantly felt at ease around him. The two struck up a close friendship, interacting in person and over time having a deep relationship with each other. She would become a well-known visitor to Joseph and happily stay in his company for hours at a time. Mrs Kendal's husband also visited Joseph on occasions, while she herself helped raise money for Joseph and his care, also sending him several gifts including many of the cardboard cutout structures he loved. As their friendship grew, she soon learnt that he was a lover of anything romantic or theatre-based so she invited Joseph along to the theatre to watch her perform. When Dr Treves heard of this arrangement he was happy for Joseph to go but knew it was going to need a lot of planning, since if Joseph was to attend he was going to have to sit away from public viewing - unseen, so as to not to draw attention to himself. This meant he would have to sit within one of the balconies up top, entering the hall quietly once the lights had dimmed, wearing clothing that could do the best at disguising his deformities. Once it was planned and a date had been set, Mrs Kendal paid for his ticket and beverages of whatever he would like, and he was quietly accompanied into the theatre hall onto the top balcony to watch the play. Along with him sat Fredrick and two of the female staff members from the hospital. It was never known what play Joseph watched that night as Mrs Kendal was performing in more than one play at the time, but it was most likely 'The Ironmaster' (1884), 'Mayfair' (1885), or 'The Hobby Horse' (1886). These shows were very popular and ongoing at St James's Theatre, running for many years. It is fair to say either way, whatever show Joseph watched that night it would have been a marvellous experience for him. For weeks after the event, he would talk about the play and every aspect of it in fine detail, as if trying to relive that moment again and again. Fredrick later talks about that production stating, "Joseph's reaction was not so much that of delight but of fascination and amazement, the spectacle left him utterly speechless. He was thrilled by a vision that was almost beyond his comprehension. The enjoyment Joseph had on that night and for weeks which followed was that of utter appreciation towards the well-performed play. He later told me, 'It was the best night of my entire life.'" It was never clear if this was the only occasion Joseph attended the theatre or if there had been other times Mrs Kendal invited him to a show. Either way, Joseph was extremely grateful and wanted to express his thanks and appreciation to Mr and Mrs Kendal. He did this by building an elaborate cardboard cathedral, which he sent to Madge Kendal and her husband. (It is highly speculated that this was the actual cardboard piece that is preserved and kept on display at the London Museum and may have even been one that Mrs Kendal bought especially for Joseph.)

Weeks leading up to that Christmas at the London Hospital, which was always a well-celebrated day, the nursing staff prepared decorations all around the wards, and gifts arrived for patients which staff decorated neatly underneath the many Christmas trees. The excitement of Christmas day always began within the early hours with a choir of sisters moving from ward to ward singing carols and giving gifts. During the morning Father Christmas would come with his elves and helpers to see the poorly kids and present them with gifts and goodies.

Midday was spent with Christmas dinner being served, turkey was chopped and plated up in all wards where the residents would sit and eat together (Joseph however because of his deformities had to eat on his ward alone). Dinner was finished off with plum pudding for dessert, and then the hospital would put on amateur entertainment in the evenings. For children, there was usually a Punch and Judy show, and the adults had the enjoyment of music and dance amongst each other or staff. On that Christmas, which was to be Joseph's last, Dr Treves asked him if there was anything in particular that he wanted for Christmas from the money he had been given off his donations. Christmas time for Joseph in the past had always been miserable with him being forced to associate with abusive, nasty, drunk individuals who most of the time took pleasure in taunting him for their own amusement but since being in the care of the hospital, the staff thought of him more as a friend, so it wasn't the case anymore. He received Christmas cards from the nurses and staff at the hospital and from the various visitors who had befriended him, along with many personal gifts which Joseph could enjoy. Joseph told Fredrick that he would like a gentleman's body care kit, he had seen the care kit while reading one of the newspapers and cut the article out to keep to one side hoping one day he could get it. Within the set there was a silver-backed hairbrush, a comb, a silver shoehorn, a hat brush, aftershave, a toothbrush and razors, there was also a small mirror but Fredrick removed this before giving Joseph the gift as he knew he didn't like to look at himself. Before Joseph arrived at the hospital, he had always been told he was ugly, unhuman, a curse from the devil, a woman's worst nightmare and more, so when he arrived on the ward it was crucial no mirrors be put in his room or were brought into his room at any time. The gentleman's kit was the perfect gift for Joseph and once he had opened it and thanked Fredrick, he wanted to use it straight away. Using the gentleman's kit became a common nightly routine for Joseph. He could be seen grooming himself at his side table in the quarters of his living space, brushing his thin, frail hair or putting aftershave on and slowly getting himself changed into the suit he wore on the best night of his life at the theatre. He could be heard as if roleplaying with himself picking up a woman and escorting her, with the mannerism of an old-style gentleman to whatever date location his fantasies thought up. This was a huge milestone for Joseph and showed how far his self-confidence and own individual personality had come. He was now seeing himself as all his friends saw him, no longer thinking of himself as a freak of nature but in fact a kind, genuine, unique man. Towards the end of Joseph's life, though his death was not linked to ill health, his health was somewhat beginning to wear him down. This could well have been another possibility why he chose to sleep in until midday, with him not having the strength to pull himself out of bed. Whatever the reasoning, on Thursday night, the 10th of April, when Joseph decided to take his normal routine walk in the dark around the hospital garden grounds, he was unaware this was to be his last stroll.

Friday 11th of April 1890, at roughly three o'clock in the afternoon Joseph was found dead on his bed. According to records, a nurse was running through her usual routine and took Joseph's meal up to his living quarters at one o'clock afternoon, knocked on the door and exchanged pleasantries, left the meal outside of his door (which is what he asked staff to do so he could retrieve it when he was ready). The nurse later stated, "When I arrived at his room we had a brief chat between the door and he seemed fine." Doctor Sidney Hodges, then-house surgeon, came down to 'Bedstead Square' for a routine call (which was the name of Joseph's living ward). He found the meal sat in the same place untouched, so he knocked on the door but heard no response. He took it upon himself to enter the room where he found Joseph lying on his bed and came to the realisation that he had passed away. An inquest on Joseph was held at the London Hospital on Tuesday, 15th April 1890. The next morning The Times Newspaper featured a full report on the topic - headlined 'Death of The Elephant Man'. Members of the public, mainly those who had been so kind to donate funds to Joseph wrote letters to the hospital sending their condolences. Among those was a lady who took a personal interest in Joseph, she wrote: "I am saddened to see in today's paper which explains that the poor Mr Merrick, the 'Elephant Man' has passed away. It is a merciful way of going out of what to him has been a very sad world, though he has received a great deal of kindness in it. Thank God he was not unprepared, he is now safe and can rest."

Although he never saw him alive again, Joseph's uncle Charles did travel down South to see his nephew for the last time and to identify the body. His aunt and uncle were the only two family members who kept in distant contact with him, sending him letters on occasion and the big donation which went towards Joseph's stay at the hospital. His father, stepmother and disabled sister on the other hand hadn't seen Joseph since he left home at the age of seventeen, nor did any of them reach out for information on him after his death. It's for these reasons that it is very likely that once Joseph had left home all of them years ago, the family simply wiped their hands of him, carrying on with their own lives and completely disregarding Joseph out of memory. Joseph was found stretched across his bed which indicated he was definitely awake and functioning, otherwise his body would have been in a completely different position. On attempting to leave his bed his head fell backwards, and he suffered the event which caused his death. The official cause of death, when Fredrick carried out a post-mortem was 'Asphyxia'. He said Joseph died of a broken neck. The thought was he died of 'Asphyxia' because his head crushed his windpipe and in the process, his head had fallen backwards breaking his neck. It was over a century later when a new theory was put forward with advantages in technologies. New tests were able to be undertaken that were restudied. The thought was instead that he died from a crushed or severed spinal cord after his head fell back dislocating under the weight of his head. Due to the disadvantage of not having the ability for general testing in the 1800s, the exact causes of Joseph's deformities were never clear, it was thought throughout the twentieth century that Joseph suffered from 'Neurological syndrome' (which is a condition where there is a problem with the functioning of the nervous system and how the brain and body sends and receives messages), but this theory was soon disregarded when it was understood that the tests Fredrick Treves undertook on Joseph were that of a stable mind and man. In late 1930, Dr Parkes Weber put forward the suggestion that bone malformations occurred as a result of the involvement in neurofibroma formation of the periosteum (which is the fibrous membrane that shapes and forms the surface layers of a bone). Next, the theory was that of 'Elephantiasis' (an enlargement and hardening of limbs or body parts due to tissue swelling) but that was deemed incorrect as this only affects body parts - leg/legs, arm/arms, hand/hands; whereas Joseph was covered head to toe in different sized deformities. In 1986, the newest theory was that of 'Proteus Syndrome' (A rare condition by overgrowth of the bones, skin, and other tissues. Organs and tissues affected by the disease grow outwards deforming the body's appearance). The thought today is that it was an extremely severe case of 'Neurofibromatosis' (Neurofibromatosis are a group of genetic disorders that cause tumours to form on nerve tissue. These tumours can develop anywhere in the nervous system, including the brain, spinal cord, and nerves). Medical professionals deem this to be the most probable cause.

There is at present no way of confirming whether or not Joseph was 100 percent a case of 'Neurofibromatosis' caused by a genetic mutation (only every 1 in 3,000 suffer from this condition, making it very rare). There is also no way of 100 percent certainty knowing what Joseph's mother suffered with or what his disabled sister suffered with were linked to his disorder, but the factual evidence does suggest the disorder was inherited as a 'Simple Mendelian Dominant Characteristic', so the disease was invariably passed down from sufferer to sufferer without skipping a generation. The only theory is the fact his mother and sister were also born with physical problems indicates circumstantial evidence for a defective gene perhaps being carried by Joseph's mother. Evidence shows that there was no illness of any kind being found on his father's side. DNA testing on Joseph's hair was taken in 2003 to test and understand the implications of the disorder, but they came back inconclusive because his skeleton had been bleached multiple times to reserve it at the Royal London Hospital for further surgeons and students to research. His life has been depicted in plays and movies showing a fascination with Joseph, if only he had been born a century or so later, things might have been very different for him and he wouldn't have had to suffer the cruel life which he did, as being displayed as nothing more than an abnormal, unhuman, strange, freak. In 1979, a play was created by 'Bernard

Pomerance', who was an American playwright and poet with his best and most known work being that of 'Elephant Man' which was a huge success portraying the hard life of Joseph. There was then in 1980, a film called 'The Elephant Man', directed by 'David Lynch' who is an American filmmaker, painter, visual artist, actor, musician, and writer. This film went on to be a huge success, then most recently in 2014, there has been another play created which plays through the period of time Joseph was living within the hospital grounds. It is performed in London, Liverpool and many more, its star guest who plays Joseph is 'Bradley Cooper', who is a famous American actor and film-maker mainly known for lead roles in 'The Hangover' Trilogy (2009/11/13), 'Silver Linings Playbook' (2012), 'American Sniper' (2015) and, 'A star is born' (2018).

Summary & Conclusion

Joseph lived a life of utter despair and misery; without a shadow of a doubt, he led one of the hardest lives ever documented in human history. In the timeframe of his life, he was passed off and seen as nothing more than a monster who had to spend his entire life trying but failing to fend off those around him, who only wanted to use him for their selfish gain or to humiliate him for their own sick pleasure. Throughout the vast majority of his adult life, he was seen as a money-making ploy - someone who should be seen not heard, used but not cared for, and thought upon as nothing more than an emotionless freak of nature who was worthless and in no way equal to his peers - his only job in life was to make money for those he was unfortunate enough to be associated with. As a child, he suffered greatly at the hands of the people who were meant to protect him. Abuse of a child in itself is a tremendously traumatic experience for any to have to cope with, which can have lifelong effects where the person from then onwards finds it hard to trust, feels hopeless, and finds it hard to function as a normal individual within society, but for Joseph, it is fair to say it would have just added to his already visual physical abnormalities and emotional problems. Joseph was an emotional person at heart. In childhood before his mother's death, he looked up to her as his role model. She was a woman whom he idolised and thought highly of. To him she was the one constant in his life whom he could rely on to protect him and guide him the way a mother should, so when she sadly passed, he never came to terms with her death but from then onwards she was stamped in his mind as the woman he adored through and through with nobody being able to compete.

From all the negligence Joseph suffered at the hands of his father, it is quite possible that his father himself suffered abuse as a child. The way Joseph Rockley dealt with many situations throughout his life would surely indicate this. He had a very low IQ, it's been proven in a lot of cases that having a lowered IQ without any forms of mental impairments usually plays a part when it comes to abused individuals, this is because in childhood the brain is still developing making it very sensitive to injury, so when trauma or maltreatment occurs this can have lifelong damaging effects which can result in lowered intellectual intelligence. In the words of Joseph himself later in life, his father was verbally aggressive towards his mother, sometimes having mild outbreaks of aggression throwing objects around, this shows somebody who finds it hard to control their emotions. This can sometimes be linked to trauma being buried in the past, which they don't know how to deal with. So they take the frustration out on objects or being verbally aggressive towards whoever is in their firing line. There is then the main factor of violence Joseph Rockley inflicted on Joseph as a young teenager. These were almost daily beatings which would continue for years until Joseph finally decided to leave for good. This is another indication that Joseph's father may have been abused as a child and is mimicking the actions he had learnt. This abuse cycle has been proven to get genetically passed down through generations making it one-third more likely that abused children go on to abuse themselves. Luckily not everyone follows the cycle, if Joseph Rockley had been abused and inflicted this abuse on Joseph - Joseph should theoretically have been angry and abusive himself but for him, it was the opposite and in fact, he was one of the kindest people you could have ever met. Sometimes certain individuals are wise enough to understand that abuse on any level is inhumane and are able to break the cycle knowing that it is never the right thing to do. Throughout his whole life, Joseph was always the opposite of what people thought of him, he was so much more intelligent and insightful than people ever gave him credit for. With everything Joseph had to endure it is astonishing how he stayed so amiable and strong-willed.

Joseph underneath all his tumours and growths was still a human being with his own feelings and thoughts. It is appalling how people didn't understand his condition, so they thought it fine to attack him for being different. That childlike behaviour is unfortunately what we all have to survive through when it comes to adolescence, kids can be cruel but they are still learning and trying to find a way to fit into the world the best way they know how. Fitting in for a child or teenager, a lot of the times comes down to wanting to feel popular, so to feel included could mean looking negatively at those who are different. Eventually, children grow out of this behaviour and start to understand that sometimes people can't change the way they are born and they should be accepted regardless. For Joseph, though he was unlucky enough to be around these shallow-minded types of bullies who later grew into fully grown adults, his father is a good example of this. Just because Joseph was different and caused extra stress to his father, it meant he was unable to cope, but rather than asking for help and doing right by his son like a good father should, he did the only thing these people know, try and attack the problem to make it go away, luckily for Joseph he was wise enough to know that he didn't deserve being abused and finally did get away, but only into the hands of yet another abuser - his manager Tom Norman. It is shocking how a middle-aged, relatively intelligent businessman could still, by his age, be so vile to a young man who quite obviously had serious health problems a lot worse than the majority of the population and even more so Tom spent a substantial amount of time around Joseph, even living alongside him in the same building. Still, when they left Europe in attempts to take their freakshow further afield to draw in a bigger audience, he was able to participate in the sickening act of beating, mugging, and abandoning Joseph, leaving him in a country he was unfamiliar with and around people who didn't speak his language.

Joseph only had a hand full of friends throughout his entire life, his mother being the main one through his childhood, brothers Dooley, and Harry Bramley who participated in the freakshows alongside Joseph when they were touring, then Dr Treves and Madge Kendal being the main through the last years of his life. Away from them, there aren't many more who looked to Joseph as a friend but rather someone they could use and abuse. If Joseph had been born today, his life would have played out so differently, not just in the sense of advances in medical understanding of his condition and being able to provide the medical attention he desperately needed, but he also wouldn't have had to spend a huge percentage of his life being looked upon as a creature not of this world. He would have been able to have been cared for by the right people - people who would have helped him in the best way they knew and made his difficult life a bit easier. We humans have come so far in our evolution that in today's society, unique individuals such as Joseph and many others all over the world who are still suffering with these horrendous conditions are no longer rejected as outcasts and treated like wild animals stripped of feelings. These people rightly so are treated with compassion and guided by professionals to a better life or at the very least a life they can live that best suits their complex needs. Sadly though, Joseph wasn't so lucky, being born at a time when these complex illnesses were frowned upon and thought of as spells cast by evil spirits or demons. People strongly believed that individuals such as Joseph shouldn't be allowed to participate in life as normal humans and in fact, they should be locked away in an abandoned institution somewhere away from all civilisation to await their death. This is why freakshows were a huge part of the culture, because people were so fascinated by these unique people. But only in the sense of viewing them as freaks and ungodly beings, not taking into consideration any of their struggles away from the shows. It was only after the shutdown of freakshows in the 1880s that people started to view them differently, finally starting to see and understand these people as humans with unfortunate, devastating conditions who need extra help and support in life rather than the mockery they were subjected to for centuries.

Joseph was a religious man, being a devoted Christian, having strong Christian beliefs. He believed Jesus is the saviour of the world, God created the universe, heaven, and earth in six days. There is a heaven where the good are at peace, and a hell where the bad pay for their sins, angels and demons roam the earth amongst us, and one should always follow in the path of righteousness. For all the terrible places Joseph found himself in and for all the hurt he suffered at the hands of others, if there is a place such as heaven then Joseph will be there with his mother resting in peace.

Was I so tall, could I reach the pole, or grasp the ocean with a span; I would be measured by the soul, The mind's the standard of the man? - Poem written by Joseph Merrick (1862-1890)

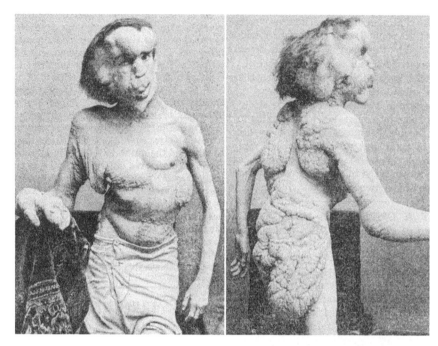

Dr Fredrick Treves   *Mrs Madge Kendal*

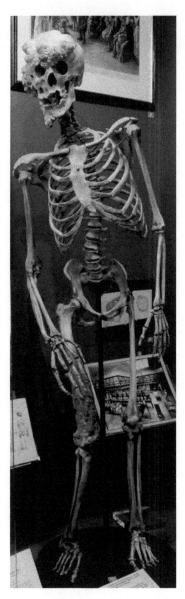

Skeleton of Joseph preserved at London Museum